Dog Meet Baby!

By MAV4LIFE®

Walk-Through of How to Introduce Your Dog To Your Newborn!

Dog Meet Baby!: Walk-Through of How to Introduce Your Dog to Your Newborn!

ABOUT MAV4LIFE®

"Mav4Life®, is the ultimate resource for dog owners. From free dog training e-books, to toys that will provide your furry friend with hours of enjoyment, we are all about the animals. Learn more on our website: www.mav4life.com, blog and keep up with the fun daily by liking us on Facebook & Instagram @Mav4LifeDogToys

Tail Wags & Sloppy Kisses, Team Mav4Life®"

Make sure you grab your Mav4Life® product today! And give your best friend the quality they deserve! For your FREE GIFT Check out our website!

Table of Contents

Dog Meet Baby!: Walk-Through of How to Introduce Your Dog to Your Newborn!

Introduction

 After years of trying, it has finally happened. As you sat there on the toilet seat, jiggling your leg impatiently as you wait for the pregnancy test to prepare itself, your mind begins to swirl as your significant other stands at the door. Or, maybe you are the one at the door, watching the questions slosh behind your significant other's distant eyes as you grip the door frame, waiting for the pregnancy test to be done. Maybe the two of you have been planning this for years... or maybe you are just beginning and absolutely petrified. Maybe this is a joyful occasion, or maybe it is not.

Whatever the scenario, just as the pregnancy test is done being administered, your beautiful furry friend comes dashing in and jumps off its feet, knocking the pregnancy test over as your furry fuzz ball bounds into your lap and begins licking your face. For a split second, you forget about the world around you as you hold your soft best friend close as a question slowly slips through your mind.

Will my dog be compatible with a baby?

It is a question you are not quite sure how to answer. Maybe your dog has never really been around kids, which could become a problem. Maybe your dog has been around other kids and not enjoyed it, which could really become a problem.

Maybe you are still figuring out if you will be good with children.

You wonder if your dog will be gentle enough, or too overprotective. You wonder if your dog will become territorial, or distant, or not like the way a child grabs harshly at foreign objects. You wonder if the dog will play too hard with the baby, knocking them down or over and unintentionally injuring your child.

Maybe you are wondering if you will be gentle enough with your own child.

You begin to think about all the late-night feedings and whether your dog's routine will be affected. You wonder if the dog will develop any animosity towards you as you walk out the door with your child and not them. You wonder if your child will try to put the slobbery doggy toys in their mouths and get themselves sick, and you start to run down all the possible cleaners in the house that you have to toss so your floor-licking little one does not make themselves sick.

Maybe you start to wonder if this child is going to make you really sick.

And then, your furry friend nuzzles up under your chin, licking you in delight as a

Dog Meet Baby!: Walk-Through of How to Introduce Your Dog to Your Newborn!

smile breaks out across your face. You hold your dog close as you sigh and open your eyes, and when you do you see that the pregnancy test is no longer on top of the bathroom counter.

Your eyes dart around frantically looking for the future-telling stick, and as your eyes descend upon its presence on the floor, you scramble onto your knees as you for the stick.

Then, grasping it as tightly as you can, you pan your eyes down to the blue plus sign on the second stick you have unwrapped and used today.

Congratulations! You are expecting a beautiful, bouncing bundle of joy.

Now what?

Chapter 1: A Doggy Disposition

A dog's overall demeanor is more manageable for an adult than it is for a child. If a dog does not enjoy public, it is easy for the adult to keep the dog indoors and rest with it. However, if a dog has gotten used to having you all to itself, then the addition of a child can rile it up. Likewise, a dog that is not used to being around new people can even become aggressive with a newborn child, placing both the child's and the dog's life at risk.

Assessing your dog's behavior is essential. Take the time to watch what they do, and take mental notes or jot down in a personal journal things you see. Is your dog an outside dog, or not? Is your dog alert around people, or relaxed? Is your dog aggressive or easily upset in specific instances? If they are, jot down the instances in which your dog becomes unnecessarily (or even necessarily) aggressive. This will help to pinpoint behaviors that will help you figure out whether your dog's natural disposition is conducive to having a child.

If it is, congratulations! If it is not, there are tips and tricks throughout this book that can aid in helping your dog adjust to this new dynamic before your beautiful bundle of joy finally arrives.

However, some families might be debating on whether to add a puppy into the family around the time the baby comes. Many people believe that adding a dog

Dog Meet Baby!: Walk-Through of How to Introduce Your Dog to Your Newborn!

around the time the baby is due to come home can increase the chances that the dog will be tame and safe around a child. However, this is not the case, and here is why: puppies are more prone to aggression in new environment than older dogs are to new introductions.

Puppies are just as territorial as full-grown dogs, and if you bring a puppy home before the baby has arrived, that puppy is going to have just enough time to mark out his own territories and ownership within the house. This means that all of the baby things you are bringing into the home in order to prepare for the arrival of your child, like toys and the nursery furniture, are going to be perceived by that puppy as theirs. This can cause a slew of reactions, such as excessive barking at your child during nap times and aggressive behavior while your newborn is swaddled in that blanket the puppy thought was theirs.

It is a good idea to have a puppy alongside a child for various reasons, as long as you can keep the issues that come with a puppy at bay. As a parent to an infant, the last thing you need to be concerned with is cleaning up a dog that overly sheds or is still not potty-trained. Consider purchasing a dog that does not shed and has already been potty-trained in order to eliminate these struggles alongside handling your newborn child.

If you want to reduce the territorial aspect of your puppy, introduce the puppy into the home after you take your child home. This means the child will be in the home before the puppy, and the puppy will regard your child as a natural entity within the home. If you bring the puppy in first, the puppy will view your child as an invader and attempt to protect your home from it. There is nothing wrong with this; it is a simple survival mechanism. However, it can harm your child and risk the life of your puppy in the process if any true damage is done.

If you want to purchase a puppy for your child to grow up alongside, get a puppy that has already been house-trained and sheds minimally -- such as a poodle or a beagle -- to minimize the work that comes with a dog. Make sure to introduce the puppy after the baby has been brought into the house. Do not introduce the puppy a day after, however. Give the newborn infant time to reside in the house and sleep in their crib. This will establish the baby's dominant scent on things that are designated for the child, and the puppy is more likely to regard the baby's possessions as items that are off-limits for it instead of attempting to take them from the baby because they have established their own personal intent.

But, no matter if you have a full-grown dog or a new puppy, there are behaviors

Dog Meet Baby!: Walk-Through of How to Introduce Your Dog to Your Newborn!

that can quickly turn problematic. If not taken care of, this can lead to injury of your child, and many states have laws that threaten domestic animal life if they threaten basic human life. There are signs and specific sounds to look for in your puppy or dog when keeping an eye out for problematic behavior, and there are even behaviors dogs can exhibit before a baby is here that should trigger a response of worry.

The good news is there are things you can do about these problematic behaviors before resulting to things like giving your beloved pet to another family. But, before you can tackle those types of obstacles, you have to know what you are looking for in your dog. Whether you see it and refer to it in your journal or are witnessing it for the first time, it is imperative to understand exactly what you are looking for.

After all, seeing these changes in behaviors could mean the difference between your dog being a family member and your dog being taken from you.

Chapter 2: When Normal Behavior Becomes Problematic

There are behaviors in dogs that we put up with as adults that are sometimes not conducive to having a child. For example, excessive barking might be an issue, but it is an issue many family members simply cope with because they love their dog.

However, that excessive barking will turn into ruined naptimes and sleepless evenings whenever a newborn infant is in the house. If your dog barks every time someone gets up to walk, or every time the doorbell is rung, or even when you get up in the middle of the night to pee, this has now become a behavior that needs to be addressed.

Another trait is sensitivity to loud noises and tactile issues. What I mean is, if your dog is easily agitated by loud, abrupt sounds and does not enjoy being petted for long periods of time, this could become problematic for an infant. Babies cry and scream in order to signal that they need something, and if this easily agitates a dog they might become aggressive with the fragile child. Not only that, but a child will use their hands to latch onto and bring anything within their grasp to their mouths. So, if a dog does not enjoy being petted roughly or even groomed, then you can only imagine their innate response when a small child latches their fingers down onto their fur coats.

There are some traits that are inherent triggers that should be looked out for immediately, however, if you understand that your dog does not like to be around children that can be a very problematic issue that is not always fixable. Also, if your dog has a history of killing other small animals, such as squirrels or birds, then you need to examine further as to whether that aggressive and dominant behavior extends towards small children.

If a dog displays aggressive acts and is easily territorial, rest assured that while it is worrisome, these are behaviors that can be corrected within an animal, whether you attempt to do it yourself or whether you seek out a professional trainer to assist you in the matter. These types of acts can stem from yanking you around while they

Dog Meet Baby!: Walk-Through of How to Introduce Your Dog to Your Newborn!

are leashed all the way to people not being able to approach you when the dog is around. Make sure you document all of this information somewhere so that, when prompted by someone, you can easily flip through and recall it.

However, if your dog cannot be left alone for long periods of time, this is something that needs to be fixed sooner rather than later. While it might seem endearing now, a dog that is unable to be alone not only is more prone to developing destructive behaviors associated with separation anxiety, but you risk the development of more aggressive behaviors when your child comes home with you. For example, if your dog is used to cuddling in your lap at night, but all of a sudden this foreign object is inhabiting your lap and is feeding on something, the dog might try to latch onto the baby's clothing or paw them out of your lap in order to reclaim the dog's rightful place in your lap.

Likewise, if your dog is very defensive of anyone in the household, this will lessen the chances of this person being able to interact with the child. Because the dog is more defensive, they might be more unwilling to allow you to hold the infant, and will become aggressive if you do so anyway.

Some people even have more than one dog. This means you have to look at these issues and document them twofold. If you have multiple dogs that do not get along, then some outside professional help will be necessary in order to retrain your dogs to be civil with one another. What does this have to do with the baby? For one, when a dog gets worked up, it does not simply leave its emotions behind it when it walks away from the situation. If a dog is more passive, it can hold its frustrations and remove itself from the situation before dispelling of those frustrations elsewhere. This heightens the chance that your dog could become aggressive towards your child if your child wants to interact and play with the dog while the dog is frustrated.

Another scenario that might take place is the child wandering into the altercation, becoming injured as a third-party casualty in a disagreement between the dogs.

There are other traits to keep your eye on that, while not at the expense of your child's safety, can simply drive you nuts once you have a newborn in the house. A newborn child takes a lot of work, and recovery from childbirth takes months. If your dog requires all of your time and attention, this can result in your dog simply being up under your feet every time you stand. This increases the risk of tripping over your dog and dropping your child, or even injuring yourself as you are trying to recuperate from the exhaustion of the new situation

Dog Meet Baby!: Walk-Through of How to Introduce Your Dog to Your Newborn!

A high maintenance dog is another worry as well. If your dog requires lots of outside and bonding time, this is going to become very hard to do with a child lounging in your arms while you are sleeping only five hours a night. Another form of high maintenance in a dog is their coat of fur and how much upkeep it takes. If you have a dog with a large coat of fur that sheds constantly, consider keeping it closely trimmed to the body or shaving it off altogether. It does not have to be permanent, but you do need to find ways to adequately split your time between your new child and your clinging dog.

The good news is that most, if not all, of these symptoms and behavior patterns can be corrected both with professional training and with tactics you can explore at home. Some of the tactics correct behaviors, in general, and some of the tactics help ready your dog for the new scenario of bringing home another human being.

Remember: if you are considering purchasing a puppy to grow up alongside your child, make sure it is house-trained, does not have a high-maintenance coat of fur, and is introduced a few weeks after your child has been home.

Chapter 3: Is Your Dog Ready For A Child?

For many individuals, obedience class is the way to go for their dog. Many do not want to take the chance that their dog could potentially harm their child, and no one can blame them. For you, that might be the exact road you need to take... and no one is going to look down on you for that.

However, you still might be wondering whether your dog is ready for a child.

If some of the behaviors above are exhibited, then your dog might not be ready. As hard as that is to stomach, that does not mean there is something wrong with your beautiful little pooch. All it means is that the new scenario your dog is about to be introduced to is too precious for simple trial-and-error. We might not go through these types of motions when moving homes or changing their bed area because you know the most backlashes you might get is a dog that is clingier than usual.

You know the backlash for moving homes is not an injured child.

However, when an infant enters the picture and territory starts to be encroached upon, it becomes a proper time to remind you that your dog, while loving and cuddly and beautiful, is still an animal with base instincts. Yes, your dog knows how to sit, stay, fetch, and play, but your dog also knows how to attack when it feels threatened, bark when it senses something new or dangerous, and kill when it feels necessary.

And that is too volatile for a simple trial-and-error scenario when it comes to bringing your child home.

If you are still wondering whether your dog is ready for the new addition to your family, the easiest way to go about figuring it out is to put your dog around other children. Get together with some friends that have children or simply ask parents in your neighborhood if it is alright for their children to interact with your dog with adult supervision. Simply explain to them what is going on.

However, if that is too nerve-wracking, or somehow sounds too odd, then take your dog to a dog park. Sit with your dog leashed and on a bench, and watch how your dog reacts to not only passing adults, but passing children. Watching their

Dog Meet Baby!: Walk-Through of How to Introduce Your Dog to Your Newborn!

interaction with other dogs is beneficial, but watching them interact with passing children will give you insight into their knee-jerk reaction: is your dog barking at the passing adults and children? Is your dog nipping at their ankles? Is your dog trying to get away to go play? Is your dog growling or baring their teeth at the passing adults and children?

The answers to these questions will give you your answer: if your dog is displaying aggressive behavior towards passing individuals, then your dog is not ready for an infant to enter the scenario. If your dog is alert, but not aggressive, than some simple tips and tricks could be employed to help them become more familiar with the situation. If your dog is completely lackadaisical and couldn't care less as to who passes them by, then congratulations! Your dog is ready for an infant.

Resolving potential behavior problems takes work. Depending on the severity of the issue, I still highly recommend seeking professional counsel. However, you know and understand your dog better than anyone, and if you feel you can tackle their behavior issues in time for the arrival of your beautiful child, then there are ways you can begin to tackle these behaviors. Sometimes, it is as simple as teaching them something new and useful, and sometimes it is as difficult as teaching them they are not the priority of the household. Either way, there are things you can implement for every aggressive and hesitant action that every dog might show in order to signal to you that they are not yet ready for the intrusion.

Remember, however: highly aggressive dogs, such as ones that have small animal killing tendencies and do not like the presence of other people at all, can be trained to a point, but their instincts cannot be inherently trained out of them. Use your own judgment for the safety of your child, and if your dog does not show enough improvement for you to feel settled about bringing your bundle of joy home, consider finding a better and more suitable home for your dog. I know, it is going to be heartbreaking, but if your dog cannot adjust to the new family dynamic, it can not only risk the health of your child, but it can risk the mental and emotional health of your dog.

Chapter 4: How To Resolve Potential Behavior Problems

There are some behaviors in dogs that should be corrected whether there is the introduction of a child or not. Behaviors such as walking in front of you when leashed are behaviors that signal to them that they are the dominant figure in the household. If you have a larger dog with aggression issues, the first step is to take them outside and run them around. While this might seem pointless, many larger dogs (like Mastiffs) have residual energy that needs to be burned. If they do not burn it, they get restless and that restlessness turns to frustration that they do not know how to get out of their system. Take them outside or to a dog park and let them run around for a couple of hours. If you have work, take it with you and get it done. This can be a relatively simple way to treat your dog's aggression if this is the root cause.

However, it is not always that easy. If you have multiple dogs that do not get along and are showing aggression, this is because there is a "pack" mentality, and one of them is trying to establish themselves the dominant head of the pack. This means that, in order to establish yourself as the "pack leader," you have to set limitations and boundaries to what all of your dogs can do. Pack mentality is simply an evolutionary advantage. Picking a pack leader means putting a dog into a selfless role whereby that dominant head looks out for the well-being of the pack. In return, the pack fully trusts the leader to make sure they are fed, kept alive, and comfortable.

In order to tame this type of aggression between your dogs, establishing yourself as the dominant pack leader is essential. How do you do this? You do it by instating boundaries and earning your dog's trust, just like any other pack leader.

For some dogs, the sheer amount of attention is the issue. So, in order to prepare a dog like this for an impending baby arrival, gradually decrease the amount of time you spend around and engaging your dog. This does not mean you have to leave them in the house by themselves, but it simply means that you will slowly taper off the attention you give them, no matter the amount of attention they are giving you. One way to start is by not acknowledging your dog when you come home from work or the store. When you walk into the house and your dog is jumping all over you to lick you, simply walk past.

While it might seem heartless, and prove to be very difficult for some dog owners, this is the first step in acknowledging to the dog that they are not the most important facet of the house and that they do no not need all of your attention. Then, you can slowly escalate it in other ways: do not always pet them when they nudge your hand to be petted and do not make a big show of it when they hop into your lap. All of these things will work to tame your dog's need for your physical show of love and it will force the dog to rely on other outward showings of love you have for him or her, such as regularly feeding them, grooming them, and taking them outside.

Another way to prepare a dog for the arrival of a child is to desensitize the dog to the sounds and smells of a child. Take your phone and plug it into a speaker somewhere and play, at low volume, the random cries and giggles of a child. It will attract the attention of your dog at first, and if you have a barker, they will bark endlessly at the source of noise. But, as they become accustomed to the presence of the noise they will begin to calm down.

And this will make naptime a lot easier on the new mom and dad.

Yet another tactic you can employ is to take your dog for a walk by a school as the children are playing on the playground or being let out. You can walk on the opposite side of the street or the same side, it does not matter. What this does is it gets your dog out and around actual children while still having a barrier in between them. Watch how your dog reacts and continue to take your dog on those walks at those same times during the day. As the presence of children becomes more normal to them, their aggressions towards the children (if any) will mellow out, thereby decreasing the chances that they will be aggressive with a newborn infant in the home.

Understand that these routines need to be altered months in advance. If you implement these within weeks of your precious baby's arrival, they simply will not work. The best-case scenario is to begin implementing these new changes to routine and sounds the moment you find out you are expecting. This will give you the greatest chance of assimilating your dog to the new atmosphere before determining whether your dog will be able to handle the new addition or not.

But, there are still things you can implement even after the baby is due to come

Dog Meet Baby!: Walk-Through of How to Introduce Your Dog to Your
Newborn!

home that can ease things for everyone in the process, including your dog. These are real-life transitional issues that many people face when bringing their new baby into a home with a dog, and you have to understand that you are not alone.

I promise that you are not alone.

Chapter 5: Real-Life Transition

When it comes time for the transition, there are some people that feel as if the work they have done is enough. Likewise, there are some people out there that feel the work they have done with their dog is not enough. Whichever side you it on, I can tell you that you still need to be implementing ways to help your dog adjust well after the baby has arrived at home.

Try to see your dog's adjustment through your own eyes: you might be getting up at night with the child and then zoning out during your days, wishing you could sleep. You might hit your first stressful moment in the home where you simply have to pass the baby off to your partner or helper who comes walking through the doors while you go and have yourself a good cry. Adjusting to a new baby is hard.

And your dog is no different.

There are some basic preparations, like making sure your dog has their own space. Just as your child has their nursery as their own space, your dog needs to have their own space as well. Corner off an area of the house, or even simply a corner, and place their things in that area. Let them designate this area as theirs and do not allow your child to enter their space.

Dog Meet Baby!: Walk-Through of How to Introduce Your Dog to Your Newborn!

Likewise, do not allow your dog to enter the baby's space, either (mainly, the nursery).

If you have not started to teach your dog to stay off the furniture, now is a good time to begin. If a dog willingly jumps on the furniture, they could inadvertently injure your child somehow. Whether your child is laying on the couch and the dog nuzzles them off, or whether the child is learning to sit upright and tips over onto the floor because of the jostling of the dog jumping up, this can lead to accidental, but devastating, moments that can cause undue stress and put your dog's life in danger.

When you are venturing home from the hospital, bring a neutral party that your dog is familiar with in order to help with introductions. If necessary, make sure that person has a hold on the dog's leash or collar, just in case any aggression occurs when you allow your dog to sniff the new infant. Watch for signs of aggression, like tensing in their back or low growling in their throats. If the situation is stressful for the dog, remove yourself and the child so the dog can calm down.

Give the dog time to smell and greet the child. If that idea makes you nervous, the give the dog something that has the newborn child's scent on it: a blanket from the hospital or a hat they might have been wearing on their head. Maximum safety dictates the dog should be on a leash when all of this meeting is first happening, but you know your dog best: if you feel a leash is not necessary, then to not use one. Just stay alert to your dog's overall signs of distress.

If you are someone who has multiple dogs, then the introductions need to happen one at a time and all of the dogs need to be on leashes. Why? Because if one dog gets worked up, they will all get worked up. Whether they are excited or threatened, a situation like this for tired parents can get out of control very quickly.

This is why the use of a mutual third-party is recommended when you are first coming home.

Making sure your dog is well-exercised before the first meeting of the child can ensure that the excess energy they might have at being anxious at your departure (or wait for your return) does not come out when you walk into the hold with a delicate child in your arms. Have someone take your dog for a walk, run, or even to a park to let them run for an hour or two.

Another thing to keep in mind is that your dog was part of the familial pact as well before the baby came along. One way to ensure the dog will not grow jealous and apprehensive of the baby is to make sure that, whenever people come over to visit the child, they acknowledge and give love to your dog as well. In the process of welcoming a baby home, do not forget about your dog. Just as a dog can experience happiness, sadness, and anger, they can also experience betrayal and a break in trust.

Throughout all of this, however, it is imperative that you continue to make sure your dog's physical stimulation is attended to. Even if it means hiring someone to come and take your dog for a walk or a run every day, if your dog can expel that unnecessary energy and frustration they are feeling towards the new arrival (and they will get frustrated, just like you will with your own child sometimes) it decreases the chances of the dog lashing out at yourself or your child.

And remember, if you have gotten to this point and your dog is still showing aggressive behaviors towards the child or towards you, then you need to remove yourself and the child immediately from the situation and seek help from a professional trainer.

Chapter 6: Tips And Tricks For A Harmonious Family

Even if the your beautiful dog takes to your child perfectly, and even if your

beautiful dog loves to cuddle with your bundle of joy and protect it while they are sleeping, there are still issues that have to be navigated, no matter the dog's demeanor. Alternative sleeping schedules, feeding schedules and frequently leaving the house for doctor's appointments can jar your dog, making them nervous and even prompting the development of separation anxiety.

However, there are things you can keep in mind when coaching and developing peace between you, your dog, and your child.

One of the things to keep in mind is to not ignore your dog. While you might have utilized that trick during your pregnancy in order to get your dog more comfortable with the lack of attention, this does not mean that your dog seemingly falls to the wayside. Make sure you still get that one-on-one time with your dog like you did before your child arrived, even if it means letting your dog snooze in your lap while you are taking a nap yourself.

Make sure to always let your dog have something that has the baby's scent on it. Changing the item every month will ensure that your dog keeps track of your child's changing scent as he or she grows and begins to experience hormonal changes. As adults, the smells our dogs pick up stay relatively the same. However, a child's smells are different. In order to make sure your dog does not become hostile to the changing scents, make sure you change that item of clothing, that blanket, or that toy out every month. The scent will change along with your child, and it will help your dog acclimate to those changing senses without becoming agitated.

Always continue to establish boundaries with both parties. Just as you might not want the dog in your child's nursery, your child should not be allowed into your dog's designated area. This boundary should always be reinforced and kept until

Dog Meet Baby!: Walk-Through of How to Introduce Your Dog to Your Newborn!

such time as you feel it can be let up. If the child wants the dog in their room when they are older, then the boundaries can fall to the wayside. Making sure your child follows these boundaries, however, will keep them safe. If your child gets their own space, so should your dog, and you cannot get upset with your dog when they become territorial over their individual space.

Teaching your child is just as important as teaching your dog. When your child hits their exploratory stage, it is imperative that you supervise every interaction they have with the family pet. This is the best time to teach them not to yank on the dog's ears, or grab their tail, or even clamp onto their fur too tightly. These are lessons on mutual respect, and are great lessons for any child to have, no matter the age.

Just as it is important for the dog(s) and the child(ren) to have separate areas, it is equally important for the dog(s) and the child(ren) to have time where they all bond together... with your supervision, of course. If everyone's naptime begins to align, try snoozing on the couch with everyone curled up around your body. If you take the baby on a walk in the stroller, consider leashing the dogs and taking them with you. If feeding times start to align, the simple act of eating together can become a wonderful bonding moment. These moments will help establish the dog's place in the pack as well as get them used to the idea of having your child around, and it will do wonders for the relationship between your child and your pets.

Another great tip is to always keep an eye out for your dog's stress reactions. Low growling, tense shoulders, and shallow panting are all signs your dog is in distress. Just as you and the child have off days, so will your dog, and it is imperative to give them the space they need when your dog is having an off day. Make sure your child is not forcibly attempting to interact with your pet whenever these signs are arising, as these are signs that heighten physical altercations that are not wanted.

One imperative tip is to teach your dog commands such as "shoo!" and "go away!" These might seem harsh, but when you are groggy and carrying around a newborn infant, a dog can easily get up under your feet in an attempt to be included in the activity or garner your attention. Teach your dog these commands for low-energy cues to get out from under your feet so everyone can stay safe.

Yet another way to encourage positive and settled behavior around the child when it comes to your dog is to reward them for that positive behavior. Some dogs do not react well to solely being punished for bad behavior, and in many cases this type of action can backfire rapidly. If your dog is spending quality time with your child and being gentle, kind, and quiet, reward them for that good behavior in order to encourage them to continue doing it.

You will mostly facilitate the relationship between your child and your dog. They will have time to interact with one another because you encourage it, and both your child and your dog will learn how to interact with one another from what you teach both of them. Keep in mind that teaching your child is just as imperative as teaching your dog, and it is these teachings that will keep everyone safe while navigating these new scenarios.

And remember, if you have attempted all these tricks and even worked with a professional to try and get your dog to be more even-tempered and it is still not working, your child's safety comes before your dog's. Find them a beautiful home where they will be better taken care of and in an environment that suits their temperament better, and let them live a full and positive life. Dog's move on quicker than humans, and if you screen for the right home, your dog will thrive just fine.

Conclusion

When a couple finds out they are expecting, there are several emotions that course through their bodies. For some, there is panic and shock and fleeting sadness. Maybe the timing is off, or the pregnancy was unplanned, or the couple's financial situation is not the best. For others, it is a time of joyful glee. Of jumping up and down and hugging each other until they are blue in the face and calling all family members to scream the news through the phone. Some are alone when they find out, others are with their significant others, and some are fearfully clutching the hand of their friend as they wait for the pregnancy test to percolate.

Whatever the situation, there should never be a worry as to whether an individual's dog will be alright in the transition.

Pregnancy is hard, and animals are innately in-tune with our emotional states. If you are tired and short of patience, your dog will latch onto that emotion. If you are saddened and depressed, your dog will sense that within you. If you are happy, elated, and overjoyed, your dog will rejoice in your presence. Some dogs fully imitate the emotions of their owners, and in this regard your pregnancy can be almost as hard on them as it is on you.

Almost.

What is imperative to understand is that, setting aside overly aggressive dogs that are set in their ways; any dog can be prepped for the arrival of a little one. After all, the instinct to care for babies runs in their DNA just as it does in ours. Dogs have a biological component that triggers a need for procreation and forwarding their species just like humans have, so barring very special and specific circumstances, any dog with any temperament can be helped in the transition that comes with having a baby.

One of the biggest things that happen with dogs when owners bring home their new bundle of joy is the fact that the dog becomes ignored. Their once-temperamental and easy-going dog has now turned into a possessive, aggressive, or possible even depressed dog, and you have no idea why. Understand that your dog was part of the pack first. Just as there should be no shortage of love given to your child, there should also be no shortage of love given to your dog.

Yes, this book suggested that you begin to wean your dog off the idea of constantly having your attention, but this aspect has more to do with their maintenance than their love. For example, there is a difference between a dog laying by your side and wanting to be mindlessly pet and a dog that needs to be front-and-center on your lap every single time you sit down. The former interaction is a friendly interaction that enables you to do other things, like hold your child, and the latter interaction is a dominant interaction that disables you from doing something, such as feeding your child.

That is the difference when it comes to the attention your dog needs to feel loved versus the attention your dog wants because they are high-maintenance.

No matter the natural temperament of your dog, you should always be wary when bringing your child around your dog for the first time. With something as vulnerable as an infant, it is always better to be safe and sorry. Remember when you first got your dog, no matter the age, and you were always watching out for them and making sure they were alright? It wasn't that you suspected there was danger at every turn; you simply wanted to be there in case there was.

The same goes for your child: you do not believe your dog will become aggressive with your infant, but it is better to be there and supervising interaction just in case it does.

The doggie tips, tricks, hacks, and guidance within this book are all subjective. Only you know your dog the way you do, and just like you will be the only one who truly knows what is best for your child, it is only you would understands what is truly best for your dog. If you seek out professional training, it does not mean you are a failure as an owner. In many cases, people will agree with hiring a professional: they are more adept at handling behavior issues, especially if those issues are aggressive tendencies, and pregnancy is exhausting. You simply might not have the energy to train your dog the way you need to.

And that is fine.

Your dog deserves a chance to have a relationship with the new addition to your family, and you deserve to try every single you thing you can in order to ensure that relationship is happy, healthy, and harmonious. Understand that there are some dogs that are simply not capable of this, and that is fine. Begin researching and finding them a home that is appropriate for their age, temperament, mental, and physical needs. Some dogs simply are not created and raised to tolerate children.

And there is nothing wrong with that.

Keep your family safe by researching every avenue, and never be afraid to ask for outside help, because when it comes to the "doggy meet baby" world, so many things can go right.

And so many things can go wrong.

Be a family on the winning side, whatever that means for your precious dog. And know that, no matter what decision you make, you are making it in the best interest of your dog as well as your family.

Congratulations on the expectation of your new bundle of joy. May your life be filled with love, laughter, respect, and trust. May your child flourish in health, may your family be close and connected, and may your dog find peace and happiness.

"Mav4Life®, is the ultimate resource for dog owners. From free dog training e-books, to toys that will provide your furry friend with hours of enjoyment, we are all about the animals. Learn more on our website: www.mav4life.com, blog and keep up with the fun daily by liking us on Facebook & Instagram @Mav4LifeDogToys

Tail Wags & Sloppy Kisses, Team Mav4Life®"

Make sure you grab your Mav4Life® product today! And give your best friend the quality they deserve! For your FREE GIFT Check out our website!

Made in the USA
Monee, IL
20 December 2023

50019196R00015